Genre Realistic Fic

MW00364368

 Essential Question
How are kids around the
world different?

Sharing Cultures

by Christopher Herrera
illustrated by Laura Jacobsen

CHAPTER I

Mrs. Gupta

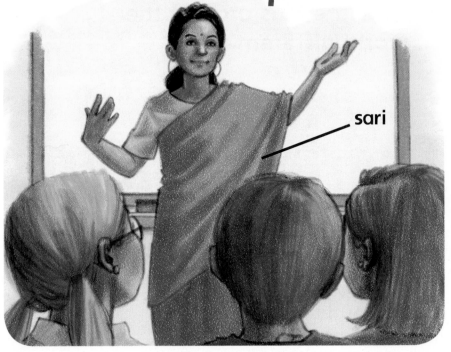

sari

Mrs. Gupta's class is surprised. They wonder why their teacher is dressed like she is.

"Good morning, class! We are going to learn about each other's customs. I'll go first," says Mrs. Gupta.

"I am wearing a sari. My family is from India. Many women wear saris there. Indians also eat dosa for breakfast. They are rice pancakes. I have some for you," says Mrs. Gupta.

dosa

STOP AND CHECK
What are some Indian customs?

CHAPTER 2

Darel and Akita

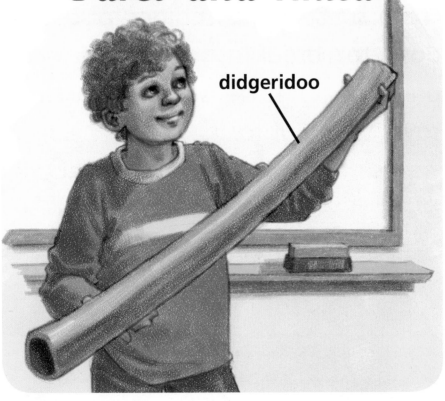

didgeridoo

The next day it is Darel's turn.
He shares a custom. "My family
is from Australia. People play
this instrument there," Darel says.
"My dad chirps like a bird when
he plays it. That sounds funny!
But I like to listen."

4

The class wonders how to play it. Darel shows them. He says, "I'll play a CD. You can hear what it sounds like."

"That's cool," thinks Alex. "But I don't have an instrument to share."

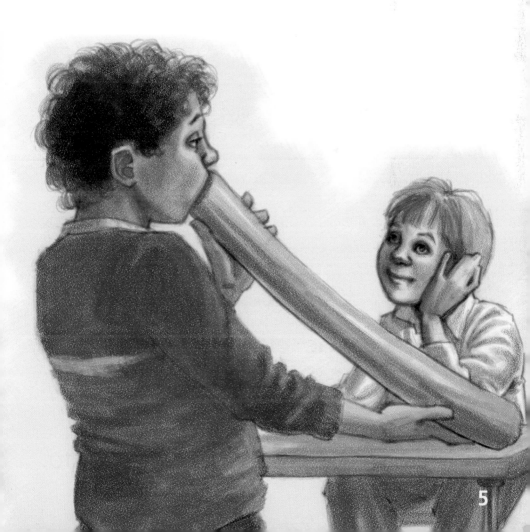

daruma

Akita tells the class about her family. Some of them live in Japan. "They give these dolls to people at New Year's," says Akita.

"People color in one eye
when they get this doll," Akita
continues. "Then they make
a wish. Suppose it comes true.
Then they color in the other eye."

"Akita has given me a great
idea!" thinks Alex.

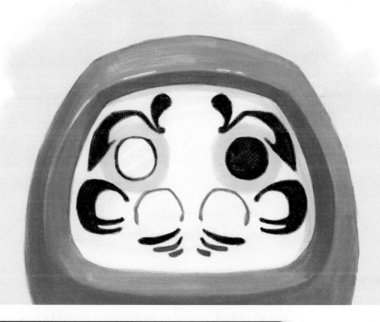

STOP AND CHECK

What are some customs
in Australia and Japan?

CHAPTER 3

Awo and Anton

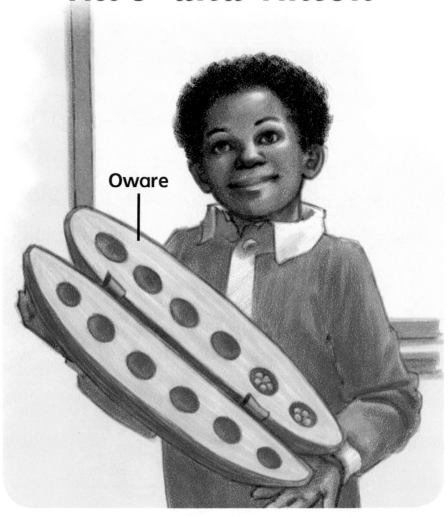

Oware

Awo says, "I am from Ghana,
Africa. We play a game called
Oware. We play with stones. We
use this wooden board."

Awo picks two people to play.
"We have to pick up all the
stones in a certain order. The
first player who does that wins."

"My father is from Russia,"
says Anton. "During the Winter
Festival, his family went to the
park. They were surrounded by
many brightly lit trees. My father
and his friends went sledding."

"Some people danced for the crowd," says Anton. "They wore colorful dress." Anton picks some children from the class. He shows them how to do a Russian dance.

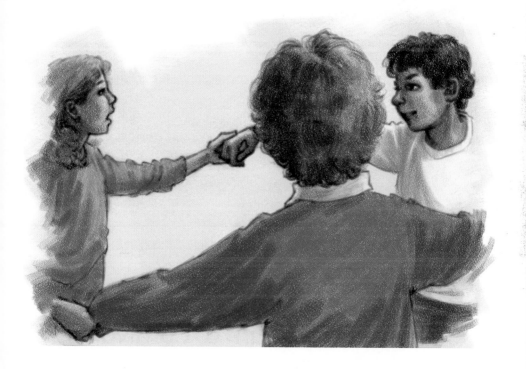

STOP AND CHECK

What are some customs in Ghana and Russia?

CHAPTER 4
Benita and Alex

Benita is dressed in a Carnival costume. She looks like a mermaid.

"My mother's family is from Brazil. Carnival is a favorite holiday there," says Benita.

"We went to Carnival last year. People were dressed up in costumes. They were part of a parade. The parade travels through the city," says Benita.

Finally it is Alex's turn.

"I am Native American," shares Alex. "My grandmother gave me this storyteller doll. See? This woman has many children. They are sitting on her lap. They are listening to her stories. Stories are important to my people. They are how we pass down our customs."

What is a custom that Akita and Alex share?

storyteller doll

Respond to Reading

Summarize

Use important details to summarize *Sharing Cultures.*

	Russia	Brazil
holiday		
custom		

Text Evidence

1. How do you know *Sharing Cultures* is realistic fiction? Genre

2. How do Alex's feelings change in this story? Compare and Contrast

3. Tell what the simile on page 12 means: "She looks like a mermaid." Similes

4. Write about two customs in this story. Use story details.

Write About Reading

Compare Texts
What are customs in different parts
of the world?

Music Around the World

Darel shared an Australian
instrument. Let's look at
some other instruments
around the world.

You blow air into a
didgeridoo to make
a sound.

In Africa people play thumb pianos. The player holds the wooden box. He uses his thumb to pluck the blades.

An African thumb piano is also called an *mbira.*

Trinidad and Tobago
steelpans

Africa
thumb piano

Australia
didgeridoo

The steelpan is a common instrument in Trinidad and Tobago. People use a pair of sticks to play steelpans.

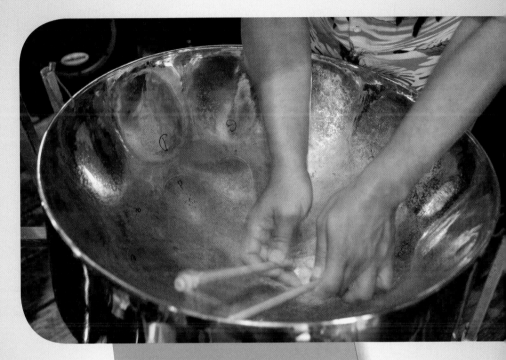

Steelpans are made from steel drums.

Make Connections

How could kids play music in different countries? **Essential Question**

Look at both selections. What are two customs in Africa? **Text to Text**

19

Focus on
Literary Elements

Characters Characters are the people in a story.

What to Look for Look at what the characters say in *Sharing Cultures.* Look at what they do. This shows what they are like. See how the characters are alike and different.

Your Turn

Think of two characters. They can be characters from another country. How are they alike? How are they different? Write sentences about your characters.